Ascent Beyond the Senses

A Spiritual Awakening

Through the looking-glass of an ascension journey

Sharon Rush

Contents

Foreword

You are a physical being, a mental being, a sexual, spiritual and cosmic being—and never in the recorded history of man have we held the potential for these dimensions of self to be more integrated and ignited.

We exist in an age that is charged with universal change and evolutionary potential. Energy is shifting on our planet and within ourselves, for we are collective energy and consciousness. As Gaia—mother goddess, essence of existence—experiences, so do we. The change can be ferocious and primal, yet when understood can liberate us to a state of wholeness, peace and personal truth.

This transition is often referred to as a spiritual awakening or ascension. While its depiction in media and social media is often one of calm introspection and reflection, ascension can be extremely challenging. It requires purging of emotional and physical toxicity and a recalibration of all that we are.

Such an event happened to me and continues to unfold to this day. *Ascent Beyond the Senses* is my personal account, which I share in an endeavour to provide reference, insight and perhaps comfort for those also going through the ascension process.

The road to becoming an awakened being can be tumultuous and sometimes dangerous. The symptoms of ascension can be misdiagnosed as anxiety, depression, hypochondria, even psychosis—or simply the result of hormones.

When I was first catapulted into this process, I was 50 years old, living in Melbourne, Australia, working as a counsellor and nutritionist, and married with two beautiful children. Life was stable, happy and fulfilling. Unbeknown to me, my existence would soon be unravelled at its core.

What unfolded threatened my life. I ricocheted from specialist to specialist, and from emergency room to emergency room. I undertook years of testing and at one stage reached a point where I struggled to go on.

Today, I often wonder how many people 'living on the edge' or experiencing what they believe to be ill health, anxiety or depression are in fact experiencing the symptoms of this evolutionary process.

I initially believed my symptoms were medical. However, after almost a year of testing on every level possible—including cellular, metabolic, structural, neurological and dental—I started developing further symptoms that defied the physical.

Although an intuitive person, I would not have described myself at the time as 'spiritual'. I was neither seeking nor coveting this experience. Professionally and personally, I had always been interested in the human experience—in personal growth and the mind–body connection. However, I pursued knowledge on a more practical level and was quite unaware of the cosmic influence on our human potential.

My experience led me to this knowledge. In my quest to survive, I researched around the clock, ultimately making a discovery that I could never have anticipated. Out of nowhere—suddenly and violently—my life as I knew it was demolished. I hungered for literature that could make sense of my experience.

I offer you my book in this spirit, writing not as a professional author but from my heart and memory—a companion to carry with you. I hope you feel understood, seen and acknowledged through your journey by reading about mine. That you never feel alone or isolated, as so many people do as they navigate this life-changing process. It took me years to find the courage to put my experience to paper.

Please note that much of what I share are physical symptoms: I encourage you to seek medical advice should any of these happen to you. It is vital to explore the physical aspects first before moving to seek a spiritual or emotional explanation.

Some people can have a gentle awakening; others are delivered a more extreme one. I know many people are confused and shaken by the changes within them. I share my journey not to exacerbate fear but in the hope that no one feels isolated in their experience and to offer assurance and solidarity.

There is meaning and purpose behind the difficulty and suffering. What's more, the experience can reward you with a sublime outcome if you trust in the miracle of it.

With love and gratitude,

Sharon Rush

My ascension experience

The beginning

Christmas Day, 2016. My life would forever be defined by this date: one reality before, one after.

Before, life had largely been happy. I was born in 1966 and was raised in a kind and loving family in Melbourne, Australia. My mother was an intuitive and compassionate person and my father solid, genuine and hardworking. I had a brother to whom I was close, three years my senior.

I grew up in the suburbs in a small house on plenty of land: time was spent mainly outdoors. They were the days before the internet—we had TV, radio and a landline phone. I walked to and from school daily, rode my bike to after-school activities and friends' houses, played sport on the weekends and loved to swim.

My early adult years, between 18 to 25, were spent working and travelling. They were wonderful times, free and full of adventure. At 25, I met a man with whom I would spend the next 28 years. We created a good life, raising two beautiful children and enjoying professional fulfilment. Life had its challenges and its pleasures, was never dull and we were always busy and full of purpose.

Then came Christmas Day, 2016.

It began on a physical level, with ringing in the ears.

After a wonderful day celebrating with our extended family, I started getting a headache. I seldom suffered from headaches, so this was unusual. But this headache was like none that I had experienced, and was accompanied by a faint buzzing in my ears. I went to bed early, head throbbing, but managed to get some sleep.

When I woke, it felt like my skull was 'fizzing'. It was as if electricity was circulating through my brain; I could hear the electricity and static in my head. My ears were pulsating with the sensation and the noise.

I took myself to a doctor. She examined my ears and found and removed some wax build-up. It made no difference: by the time I went to bed that evening, the noise and the sensations continued and it took some time to fall asleep.

By morning, both the noise level and the sensation had increased. The pulsating in my head was severe and the buzzing in my ears now sounded like a distant house or car alarm. I felt unnerved by the constant noise. Day after day, the volume and intensity increased.

By New Year's Eve, it was as if a house or car alarm were screaming in my ears day and night. The electrical feeling had also increased, and I had the sensation of 'sparks' shooting through my head spasmodically.

In one week, life as I knew it had altered. The continual noise was robbing me of my peaceful connection with the world, which was now filtered through screeching alarms that wouldn't stop. It all happened so suddenly: in retrospect, I believe I went into a type of shock.

Sleep was extremely difficult. If I somehow fell asleep through the noise, my brain would have one of its jolts of electricity and wake me up. From New Year's Eve onwards, I was sleeping two to three hours per night and often would not sleep at all. I would sometimes get up in the middle of the night and walk for hours under the streetlights to pass the time and distract myself from the nightmare I had suddenly found myself in. (Mercifully, every week to ten days or so, my body would succumb to a deep ten to twelve-hour sleep.)

My family researched and tried all sorts of white noise to play overnight in the hope that it would drown out the alarms. I started taking melatonin and herbal sleeping tablets, but nothing could silence the continual inner alarm.

These symptoms were accompanied by an inner panic. Not only had my peace, sleep and reality transformed overnight, but there was also a feeling of inner change in my emotions. It felt like a blackness—like death. Like the life I'd known was gone. Every day I tried to block out the growing negative emotions and incessant noise and focus on my 'recovery'.

My natural inclination was that something was physically wrong with me, so this was where my energy was directed: I wanted to ensure my body was working optimally to support my emotional state. Keeping my mind on practical matters was also a way to keep sane and grounded.

I had built an alliance with some amazing practitioners whom I had worked with over the years. These general practitioners (primary care doctors), nurses and chiropractors, along with my family, were my rock. Luckily, they had known me for years or decades, both personally and professionally, and supported me in every way.

At this stage, I assumed I had an extreme case of tinnitus and requested consults with an ENT to check my ears. I also requested a brain MRI with a neurological follow-up. The ENT found nothing that would contribute to tinnitus and my MRI was clear.

I then worked with both a chiropractor and physiotherapist to ensure that nothing structural was causing my condition. I had X-rays of my spine and neck (normal), had a few adjustments and started on stretching and strengthening exercises prescribed by the physiotherapist.

While I felt relieved to be getting the all-clear, I was also frustrated that there was no clear diagnosis. No diagnosis meant no remedial protocol.

All l could do was ground myself into my day-to-day routine with my family, and where possible my work, while shrill alarms screamed in my head. My family and routine kept me going and reminded me of my former self.

Through this period, I felt like I was imprisoned behind glass, watching my life play out around me but unable to touch it. I was trapped behind a wall of urgent noise that no one else could hear. Everyone's lives were playing out in their usual way at their usual pace. From their viewpoint, I looked and was the same person, my pain and torture invisible.

I felt caught between two worlds: I was in my home, surrounded by my everyday things and everyday activities, yet I knew that I had been plummeted into another world. It felt surreal.

Then it escalated.

Assault by the senses

The sounds now varied between screaming alarms and whistling, like a tea kettle, shrill and urgent.

There was one new development which was a welcome change: occasional music playing in my ears. This would range from country-and-western to electric guitar to classical. None of these were genres that I normally listened to. The music was clear but distant, nothing that I had ever heard before, and the country music and rock music always had someone singing indecipherable lyrics in the distant background. (To be clear: none of these alarms, noises or music ever came from the outside—they were sounds heard within my skull, and even heard within my body.)

I sought a second opinion from another ENT—all clear. This ENT explained, however, that hearing music could be a form of tinnitus, in which the brain tries to make sense of random sound and organise it.

I moved on from tinnitus as the explanation however when my next symptom arrived.

I started to develop visual disturbances.

At times when I was outside, I saw what appeared to be snow or light rain falling. I first noticed it when I was taking my children to school. We walked outside and I remarked that the light rain almost looked like snow and how beautiful it was. My children told me that it was clear: there was no rain or snow. I saw this vision often thereafter, even on sunny days.

My night vision also changed completely. Instead of seeing dark with some light, or shadows, everything was static—like you would see on old television sets. There was often a similar static noise in my ears.

I felt an increased sense of dread and lack of control at these developments, although they were not particularly disruptive. Another change, however, was devastating. Whenever I closed my eyes, darkness eluded me. This sanctuary was gone, replaced by flashing lights—sometimes like a kaleidoscope, sometimes colour fading in and out or spreading like ink on a page. The worst were the sparks of light, which along with the jolts of electricity in my head, would wake me up as if someone had shined a bright light in my eyes—or as if I had been struck by lightning.

By this stage, my mental health was suffering. I was severely sleep-deprived and controlling inner panic and anxiety. I became terrified to go to bed. The distraction of the day with the people I loved was my lifeboat—my connection to an old reality that made sense, a reminder of a life that I loved so much. Nighttime, however, was just me with my symptoms. What used to be my comfortable bed now felt like an instrument of torture. I fought hard to keep my sanity as I tried to fall asleep with these incessant electrical sensations, screaming alarms, colour and light, accompanied by a feeling of panic and death.

Looking back, I can see that something was bursting into life through all its mediums while simultaneously my old energies were being dismantled. In the eye of the hurricane, however, and in complete ignorance of my circumstance, I was fighting to stay alive.

My symptoms persisted and by April 2017 it was now my life mission to understand what was happening physically. I continued to explore every physical avenue possible to 'fix' my body and what I considered at the time to be my ailing health.

Day and night were spent researching and reading papers and medical information. I studied the brain and the nervous system in a vain but desperate attempt to find answers. It was the only way to feel some power over my condition—to feel as though I was in the solution, instead of drowning in the problem.

The most frustrating aspect was constant speculation by medical professionals that 'perhaps it was stress'. I had experienced stress before; to be told that what was happening was due to stress only made me feel more isolated and alone. I wished that for one moment, someone could trade places with me and experience what life was like inside my body. I was claustrophobic within my own system. Trapped in a nightclub with no exit door while trying to function in a peaceful, orderly world outside.

My next step was the dentist. I had one back tooth removed and all my mercury dental amalgams replaced by a holistic dentist, to assist in removing heavy metals from my system. I also had

IV treatment to detox heavy metals lest they were disrupting my nervous system.

Meanwhile, the lack of sleep and crying was affecting my eyesight, and I developed styes on my eyes. These were sometimes so large that I couldn't fully open my eyes.

Although I continued to function, I was overcome by a sense of grief that at times would come out in bouts of sobbing that I could never predict. I missed my life and my health, my sleep and the trust that I used to have in my body and my power to manifest my own reality. In a way, I felt kidnapped—kidnapped by a bully who was running my life. Tormenting me daily. Screaming in my ears and shining torches in my eyes.

I fought each day to be a loving, present mother, but at times my children noticed me looking tired or caught me crying. I just wanted to feel that familiar feeling of sitting with my daughter, watching our favourite show on television, or of chatting with my son, free to focus on the moment—but it was like trying to feel normal in the middle of an assault or an attack. I was in 'full fight-or-flight' mode while trying to seem normal so as not to scare those around me.

I communicated to them as honestly as possible what I was experiencing in the most appropriate way. To me, my symptoms were terrifying: 1 certainly didn't want to scare them with the details. They knew that I loved them and that I was fighting for an answer to my situation, focusing on the solution and not the problem. That was all I could give them at the time.

I felt extremely sensitive to energy, and although I continued to care about people, having time alone became crucial. Socialising was difficult to impossible. My sensitivity to energy, in addition to my exhaustion from lack of sleep, heavily dictated who I could spend time with and for how long. It also limited what activities I could get involved in.

Sensory overload occurred quickly and often. Crowds and loud noises were extremely uncomfortable. I became sensitive to smells and toxins. Perfumes, household cleaners and many other artificial chemical odours made me nauseous. This made air travel extremely difficult, so I was no longer motivated to travel. Even filling my car with petrol would leave me feeling sick for hours. Heavy energy or negativity of any kind, including ego-led behaviour, was uncomfortable to be around or even watch in movies.

These symptoms remained constant until July, when new symptoms were added to the mix, taking me to another level of suffering. It was as if I had been given time to adjust to this new reality before another was thrown out to challenge me further.

Exhaustion, and an exhaustive search

I began experiencing vibrations that would move through my body from my feet up to my head. These were joined by electricity that would surge through my body, particularly throughout the night. Rushes of energy and electricity assaulted my system like an internal motor was running and I was some kind of electrical conduit or vessel. At its peak, the vibrations felt violent, like they were frying my brain and body. I would burn up and sweat profusely. The combination of heat and waves of electrical activity would leave me exhausted, and each morning I would vomit or have diarrhoea.

I was also experiencing unexplained injuries and bruising, particularly after I managed to sleep for a few hours overnight. Bruising was random but frequent over this period. Sometimes the bruises were light, at other times large, deep and painful—bruises that would take weeks to heal. For about six months I would wake with a crushed feeling in my left hand. My finger bones on that hand cracked when I tried moving them in the morning. It was painful and my hand felt out of alignment; it too was often bruised. It would take until around midday for my hand to feel coordinated and move freely.

By this stage, I was back and forth endlessly to hospital emergency rooms overnight. I went to different hospitals, as I felt that staff would otherwise get to know me and think me insane. Each episode left me feeling depleted and drained. Doctors were unable to do anything for me, except run blood tests and offer sleeping pills or pain killers—both futile. I was so desperate: I was reaching out for a miracle to relieve me of the hell I found myself in.

I loved my life—I cherished it—but l began to question whether it was worth living in the state I was in. A few family members and my closest practitioner were the only people I could fully open up to about my vast array of strange symptoms, and how I was feeling.

I wanted to protect my children from the details, so told them little. They have since grown up and have developed an understanding of the subject. I didn't even consider disclosing my situation to colleagues as I was embarrassed. I thought I would lose all credibility if I opened up about what I was going through—even though I knew I was completely sane and grounded. I had no history of anxiety or depression; at the same time, I hadn't been focused on spirituality, so I wasn't seeking anything along those lines. Spirituality was not on my radar screen, I was learning as I went along.

My new symptoms sent me running back to my colleagues for more testing. Was it a vitamin B12 deficiency? Hormonal imbalance? EMF (electromagnetic field) sensitivity? I read endlessly on these possible causes, addressing each in turn with B12 shots, bio-identical hormones and hardwiring the house for Wi-Fi to avoid EMF exposure from Wi-Fi routers. We also installed a triple filter for cleaner water to drink and shower in. My house had become a wellness centre.

By this stage, I had been tested for everything. Neurological, genetic, cellular, structural, dental, digestive—just to name a few. Yet every day it continued: the alarms shrieking and music in my ears; the blinding lights and colour in my eyes; the burning, vibrations and electricity through my body; as well as fevers, diarrhoea and vomiting.

The more I researched my symptoms, the more the internet would deliver me articles about 'ascension' and 'ascension symptoms', 'awakening' and 'kundalini'. (Indeed, an integrative specialist I had seen in the beginning of my journey had stated plainly, 'It is spiritual.' Of course, I hadn't been ready to hear that.)

By now, almost a year since my turning point on Christmas Day, I had explored my physicality on every level, to no avail. So— should I open myself up to this being a *spiritual experience?*

The choice was made for me—or perhaps, as I have come to learn, my higher self made it for me.

Beyond the physical

My symptoms started taking on unusual expressions beyond the physical. Occasionally during the night or when my eyes were closed, I saw images, instead of just colour.

Faces mainly, of many cultures, with a particular focus on the eyes. The images were dark and dreamy and in black and white. Other recurring images included bones, as you would see in an X-ray, and foetuses, as you would view them through a scan, floating in the womb.

On two separate occasions I saw a red earth and once an image of what looked like a small German or Austrian chateau, half covered in snow. These were the only images that appeared in colour.

I can't say that any images had any significance or application. They appeared to be random—unless I am yet to appreciate their meaning.

Once as I was walking outside, I saw the word 'moringa' in mid-air. I researched moringa and discovered it was a herb. I ordered it online and started taking it. I could only assume that this was why I saw the image of this word.

I started feeling 'energy' all around me. From the earth beneath my feet particularly. Often during the night, the feeling of energy rising beneath the earth was palpable. I would walk out into the garden, grounding my feet and 'feeling' the earth's energy beneath me and around me.

Occasionally, however, the feelings that arose were terrifying—feelings of complete horror and dread, emotions that I had absolutely no connection with, had never experienced before and did not relate to. They were almost unbearable and would lead to me vomiting in the garden. This would provide instant relief.

Yet this cycle of feeling horror, fear and death, then 'vomiting them out' became a daily occurrence. Sometimes after these episodes I was so depleted it was a struggle to get back into the house. The following day my muscles would ache and my throat was so sore it was difficult to swallow.

I was also vomiting from the electrical impulses overnight, so I was losing weight and was constantly exhausted and dehydrated. Often there was nothing in my stomach to bring up, so I would dry-retch.

Sometimes I would allow the anger in. This was violent and brutal and I felt tortured and wretched every day. Yet somehow I knew instinctively, when that moment of anger would pass, that this was about something so much bigger than me that I couldn't leave it—couldn't abandon this process, this life.

There were other times when waves of emotion would overwhelm me. Frustration, rage, compassion and sadness were felt in such extremes.

I remember waiting at a stop light in my car in front of a primary school one morning. I saw a young boy of around six or seven who appeared developmentally delayed. He was with a woman I assumed was his mother. She was clearly distressed and yelling at him to leave the car and go to school. He reluctantly stepped out and stood on the pavement in tears as his mother drove off, clearly frustrated and unable to cope.

He was very thin and pale and his lifeforce energy seemed so depleted. He looked lost and frightened. The sight of this boy on the kerb, so helpless and vulnerable, unleashed deep feelings of compassion, for him and for every vulnerable soul on the planet. I carry this little boy's image with me to this day—he touched me so deeply. Sometimes, for days I would sob when I thought of him.

I am a compassionate person by nature, but this was something else. Like a tap had been turned on and there was no way of turning it off. Animals, babies, children—anyone or anything that was vulnerable or at the mercy of others made my heart feel broken. Every emotion was extreme; I felt out of my depth and unable to regulate.

I started thinking more about escape. I wanted to be alive; I loved the people in my life. But I increasingly felt the burden of my situation. Every day I felt sick, like a raging flu was in my body 24/7. I couldn't sleep or truly be in the moment with anyone, or enjoy any moment for what it was.

I was exhausted, drained and confused, and felt assaulted and battered by a violent assailant who screamed in my ear constantly. I felt like a vessel for electricity, heat, sickness and horrific emotions, none of which I felt belonged to me. The grief that I felt for my old life was destroying me.

I started seeing psychics as well as doctors, looking for answers in every direction possible.

A turn in the road

One night as I lay awake my son called home. It was around midnight. He was out at a party in the mountains, an hour from home. His friend who was designated driver was unable to drive them and he couldn't book an Uber or taxi from where he was, so he called asking if I could collect him.

As I drove into the hills, I thought how easy it would be to drive the car off the road. I was crying, wondering whether what I was experiencing was burdening everyone else's life as much as mine.

I had been such a vibrant, energetic person and now seemed to have transitioned into this strange version of myself—someone who was struggling and constantly sick. Would everyone be better off without me? My son, who was 18 at the time, had experienced many more years with me as I used to be , but my daughter was only 13, and I agonised over the thought that she may start forgetting her loving Mum.

I felt grief-stricken at the worry my situation was causing my entire family. I longed for who I used to be. It was my lowest point; I could barely see in front of me and as I went around a bend l thought about running my car off the road.

What followed is hard to describe. I saw the face of my son and daughter and felt an overwhelming sensation of love—physically, through every cell of my being as well as outside my being, like I was enveloped in a bubble.

My thoughts went to my son needing a ride home—he was waiting for me, trusting that I would be there for him. Meanwhile, my daughter would wake in the morning, trusting that her mother would be there to journey with her through another day.

In my most wretched, tortured state, love intervened. The images and feelings—many, varied, deep and profound—occurred in a split second, as if time was suspended for that moment. I didn't feel any of my symptoms; in fact, I felt that I left my body entirely.

The mountain roads were narrow and there were few places to pull over. I soon pulled into the nearest dirt driveway, shaking and sobbing. My tears came from a different place than usual—a place of feeling loved and watched over. In that instant, I had been given a renewed sense of purpose and clarity.

I believe I was delivered a miracle. It was not my time to leave, not even close.

This moment opened my mind and my heart and left me feeling entirely altered. I suddenly wondered if this entire experience was a gift of some kind. What if this bizarre, unexplainable situation was a re-birth into something new, something wonderful?

The spiritual aspect of what I was experiencing began to crystallise. I felt a new resolve to accept the physical elements and stop re-testing for things that had already been confirmed as non-existent. Instead, I resolved to embrace the experience and surrender to it. To explore the hidden gift and stop resisting and running from it.

In my counselling work, I would often share with clients that resistance is exhausting, as is the inability to accept change and evolve with the flow of life. Yet here I was doing just that—resisting what may be a miraculous event, no doubt shared by others around the world.

I picked up my son and felt so much love and gratitude to feel his hug, and to listen to the events of his evening as we drove through the mountains back home. I was struck by the beauty and perfection of the night, and felt so grateful to be a part of it.

To be denied that moment with him was unthinkable. We can never imagine the journey ahead, the guidance that we will receive, the learning yet to take place. Nor the love, hope—even the sadness, despair and grief that are all part of life's rich tapestry. We cannot interrupt our story; only through its full unfolding can we make sense of it. Only then does its greater meaning emerge.

I had taken a turn down a new road: I would explore the realms of my situation from a spiritual perspective, with a renewed sense of life and optimism. I felt cradled, protected and guided now and had full trust in the purpose of my experience.

More than real

The following morning, I questioned myself further on why I had been so resistant to exploring the spiritual avenue.

Firstly, I realised that I had fallen victim to my primal fight-or-flight response, which equates stress, fear or pain with a threat to survival.

If we rely only on our reactive brain, however, we fail to recognise painful experiences as something that can take us deeper into our soul's journey and learning. So often what appears to be problematic is in fact guiding us towards growth: opportunity disguised as destruction, embracing the pain as the path to growth.

This could come in the form of the end of a relationship that was in fact quietly abusive and holding us back; losing a job that was mundane and predictable, stunting our intellectual and social growth; a disease that woke us to appreciating life, being consciously aware of its beauty in every moment.

I now know that what I was experiencing was progressive pain. Birth, growth and recalibration can all feel painful, but this pain can sometimes offer positive change beyond what our current state of being can recognise.

Secondly, I realised that, while I had initially believed that I was ill and in need of medical care, my ongoing denial of the spiritual was more to do with embarrassment. I felt that to embrace a spiritual perspective would rob me of my professional credibility. I am now embarrassed to have felt that way! To deny our spiritual and cosmic selves, our connection to the divine plan, and downplay the truth in our lives and ourselves is a travesty.

I clearly needed to face my ego and embrace who I was becoming, be humble towards it and learn from it. From that moment on the mountain, when I accepted and surrendered, events and people entered my realm and changed the course of my life.

One of these people arrived in a shopping centre, of all places, about a week later. The lights, noise and music from the complex competed with my inner version of these, so while my daughter went into a shop, I took a break in a café opposite and ordered some mineral water.

As I sat there watching my daughter in the shop, a woman approached. She was tall and slim, very attractive and well dressed—she reminded me of the actress Jane Fonda. She asked if she could sit down next to me and I offered her a seat. I felt a sense of anticipation, like she was about to tell me something important.

She did. She told me that, 'as strange as it may sound', she read energy fields and noticed mine from outside Portmans (a store about fifty metres from where I was sitting). She said she almost ignored it and went back to her hotel, but that she knew I needed to hear from her.

'You must be going through hell, your energy is so chaotic,' she said. 'I needed to let you know that although it must be hell, you'll be OK.'

Something inside me collapsed; I grabbed her hand and burst into tears. To hear her voice my pain, my battle, which was unmeasurable in medical terms, was so validating and liberating. I felt understood for the first time since the symptoms started. I felt seen. Her understanding and insight meant the world to me.

She told me she was a real estate agent visiting Melbourne for the week. She had had a somewhat similar experience 20 years ago and now lives with seeing people's energy constantly. She saw it as 'squiggly lines and crazy shapes', but rarely told anyone as she felt that few would understand. I completely understood: this was my fear also.

I will be forever grateful to this woman for taking the time to stop and connect with me. My interaction with this wonderful stranger reminded me of the integrative practitioner I had seen who had diagnosed my symptoms as 'spiritual' early in my investigations. I decided to make an appointment to see her again.

Called from the waiting room into her office, I immediately said, 'Hello Margaret, I don't suppose you remember me?'

She countered that she did, then added with a smile, 'The universe is shaking you up.' We met and spoke often after this visit, further researching my physical and spiritual health. My visits to her clinic gave me enormous clarity. Not only did she help me cope with my symptoms, but she was a living, breathing example of a practitioner who embraced spiritual teaching as part of her practice.

She told me she had gone through something similar, which is why she recognised it so readily the first time I visited her office. 'You are going through an awakening process,' she said. 'Don't fight it.' Her words echoed that of the real estate agent I met in the shopping centre just weeks prior.

I eventually came to appreciate these words more fully, for as you venture down this road, you develop a radar of recognition for those on the same path.

These two wonderful women gave me the strength and fortitude to enter this phase of my life and embrace every weird and wonderful facet as a gift—including the insights, downloads, images and energetic impulses that it brought with it.

Once I had surrendered, I realised how exhausting the resistance had been. I replaced the exhaustion with curiosity and excitement, opening myself up to the phenomenon, eager to learn everything that I could.

I knew what was happening was significant. Even though it felt surreal, it was more real than anything I had ever experienced.

Sexual energy, relationships and connections

The extreme symptoms lasted until early 2018, just over a year after the ringing started in my ears. I stayed true to myself, however, approaching them from a more open viewpoint. As a result, I learned a great deal. By around February, my symptoms had taken on a quieter tone. In retrospect, I believe my body had needed to detox old emotions, energies and physical toxicities to allow for a lighter body energy to enter.

Audio was now a light humming in the background, almost like a hive of bees in a distant field. The electrical impulses and vibrations remained, but with far less intensity. The daily vomiting stopped, but when dealing with or witnessing intense emotion, I would often still need to release it this way. My night vision was still altered and I continued to see static; I also continued to have occasional visions and see colours when my eyes were closed. My body continued to feel extremely sensitive to toxicity, both physical and emotional, and I also had strong physical responses to weather changes.

The electricity in my head was there, but fainter, and the lightning bolts had stopped. The feelings of horror, dread and death had ceased. My feelings of 'energy beneath the earth' remained and expanded into a greater feeling of connection to all the elements and to nature generally. All the sensations and feelings described above remain to the present day.

I thought I was out of the woods. 'OK, this is where it sits,' I decided, thinking for a moment that I was now master of my fate.

Then the sexual element of my ascension started.

When reading about kundalini rising, this element is mentioned in many texts. Sexual energy is lifeforce energy, emanating from our sacral chakra, the home of our sexual and creative energy, which is truly one and the same. Orgasm is, after all, the creative force behind human life on the planet.

This energy can be transmuted and directed towards any activity—not just the sex act—making it the driving engine behind creativity, progress, passion, ambition and love. In its ideal, orgasm is the heightened expression of love in its most divine form. It has long been written in many ancient scriptures that orgasm connects us to the divine forces and to source energy; it is a connection point to the god within and to the core of our creative selves.

Awakening symptoms vary from person to person. Mine now took on a highly sexual tone, and as with all my prior symptoms, this element became extreme, invasive and life-altering. It once again felt like it came *through* me and not *from* me, so I felt hijacked by it and resentful all over again.

The challenge to be open to these symptoms and work with them, not against them, also started again. I was better equipped to handle what was happening now—I was no novice—but at the same time after more than a year of difficulty, I had assumed that peace was ahead. Looking back, I realise this was also a lesson in acceptance and tolerance.

These new symptoms started with my usual waves of vibrational energy, which always came from the soles of my feet and moved upwards through my body. These waves had subsided in severity, so they were not only more comfortable, but even felt like beautiful movement, like bubbles moving up through a glass of lemonade in slow motion.

However, the sensation altered. As the 'bubbles' moved up through my body, every nerve ending would tingle. This meant spontaneous orgasm every time the bubbles passed my pelvic area. This would happen regardless of arousal; I was most likely not thinking about sex—it was like my body was functioning separately from my mind. It was a beautiful feeling though, incredibly peaceful as well as pleasurable, and I initially revelled in the fact that perhaps I was being rewarded for all my hard labour and suffering!

As with all my previous symptoms, however, this too ended up playing out in the extreme. Arousal rose over the weeks to the point of pain in my lower abdomen. Blood was constantly pooled in my pelvic area, and I sat on the brink of orgasm constantly. At its peak, I had to relieve the tension several times a day. As soon as I had climaxed, however, within minutes the energy would return. It was excruciating.

There were very few people with whom I could share this information. I knew that for most, it would seem amusing at best. I had already held back because I was worried about losing credibility—but these latest symptoms were so personal. The isolation was one of the worst aspects. Every symptom was invisible. It had always felt like my own private nightmare.

The feeling of sexual energy was not just contained in my abdominal or genital area. It came up from the soles of my feet, and I felt it throughout my entire body. It was a powerful feeling, connecting me with energies outside myself. The energy that came with this level of arousal was not just about sex—it was about my relationship with *time*, and this had a profound effect on my life and continues to do so.

The sexual energy could only be described as *fast*, like a hurricane whirling within my system. Time felt sped up within my body. As a result, to deal with day-to-day tasks was to live in glacial slowness. I felt agitated much of the time, in a way that was driven by sexual arousal, but on reflection wasn't about sex at all.

My mind would also race ahead and my ability to read the environment and people was dramatically heightened. What was unfolding through events often unfolded for me way before they played out. It was like life was a movie I had already filmed, and now I was watching it again on the screen.

The constant sexual agitation was very invasive, and I had no real outlet. At times I had to relieve the sexual tension; however, in many ways this was futile, as it was back within minutes at full force. My internal energy seemed to have nowhere to go. At times I felt like tearing into my skin from frustration. The internal clock of my system and life as I was living it were no longer in tune.

This shift in sexual energy, its need for expression and the reorientation with time that it brought to me changed my attunement with everything and everyone. By extension, my ability to tolerate anything but my truth became impossible. I could no longer deny feelings of anger or injustice or be held to ransom, toe the line or take on anything that did not resonate with me. It was as if my tolerance was pushed to the limit and there was only room for genuine alignment.

All my feelings of pleasure, rage, love, compassion and empathy were heightened to the extreme. It seemed that anything I had suppressed—any feelings that I had put in a box to socially survive in the life that I had set up for myself—dissolved.

The feeling had a sense of urgency, and as a person who had always been there for others, this forced me to focus on myself equally now. For the first time, I turned to certain people in my life for the same level of emotional support as I had given them.

I was changing and going through a physically, sexually and emotionally tumultuous and confusing time. My usual role in life had altered.

My relationships inevitably changed. Many relationships ended, but many new ones were formed. The relationships that came to an end were an enormous source of grief, as I valued those people in my life. But as time went on, I accepted that if they ended, they *needed* to end, for both of us. Our energies were simply no longer aligned. It was time to surrender these relationships with gratitude and to work through where love truly existed in my life.

The sexual element of my ascension has thus far taken six years to work through, research and understand to the best of my ability. No doubt I have not even scratched the surface on its origin, meaning and effect on a soul level. However, we are born from ecstasy, ecstasy is lifeforce, so on some level we are ecstasy in motion.

My ongoing experience of it on a personal level is that it 'supercharges me', connecting me with an energy that gives me insight and deep connection to the world around me. If I hold the vibration without discharging it, this heightens even more. On the odd occasion when my libido has not been as high, I notice a dulling of these states in comparison.

In my attempt to understand this element of my ascension, I tried to fully embrace my heart, intuition and logic. This meant dissecting my usual response to sexual arousal. Sexual arousal was different now; it connected me energetically to my surroundings. It gave me clarity and a feeling of strength.

Over time, I have learned to hold the feeling and transmute it, using the energy to connect me to a deeper understanding of self and as a result, a deeper understanding of the people and events around me.

Surviving and thriving

I have learned so much about my experience over the past ten years, leading me to become fascinated by the human body, psychology and spirit, and their relationship and balance within us.

Ascension (awakening) is an ongoing and ever-changing process—certainly more of a journey than a destination. Over the years, the wonderful people whom I've met on this path all agree that the more you know about ascension, the more you know you don't know! The more experiences you have in this space, the more infinite the experiential possibilities become.

Surviving and thriving as an ever-awakening being in a human body remains an enormous challenge. The psychological disorientation and sensitivity to frequency and energy can make life euphoric one moment and extremely challenging the next. Planning ahead is difficult. You are driven to strive to the greatest heights, yet the smallest thing can make you collapse.

The ascension process takes place on a higher level and a human level simultaneously. The horrific biological effects I experienced—the burning up, vomiting and electricity—were no doubt about release. That is, about clearing old cells, built-up toxins, emotions and suppressed energy—a type of autophagy.

Additionally, the black dark feelings may represent toxic emotions such as ego, fear and violence. They may also represent trapped feelings from this or past lifetimes that require cleansing from the system.

This is truly an exercise in accessing your intrinsic values, as all extrinsic rewards seem to abandon you. No matter how well you eat or exercise, your body will continue to lose or gain weight and feel unwell, fatigued or overstimulated. No matter your sleep routine, your body may refuse to sleep, or you may need to sleep for fourteen hours straight. No matter how positive your attitude or how many goals you set, outcomes seem manifested for or through you, not by you. No matter how you try to feel about other people or adapt to situations, your will to make that choice seems muted and suddenly you just feel how you feel, seemingly without control.

The natural law of cause-and-effect seems to have left the building, and all the rules no longer apply.

The 'self' that you had engineered to function within your world dissolves, and in its place a powerful force has awakened that guides you from a deeper inner core. No more smoke-and-mirrors, no more playing it safe. Sovereignty and authenticity are the only options.

The long-term effects of this can vary. For some, this shattering of the ego self is devastating, and adapting is impaired by lack of knowledge and support or by impaired mental or physical health. For some, the changes may engulf them in grief, shame, financial or personal loss, mental health issues or isolation.

This is why support during this time is crucial. On a personal level, I could never have conceived that a human being could have such an experience until it entered my life. That such a force could evaporate everything that I knew to be solid, factual and real. My bodily functions, control of my feelings, my energetic connection with the environment were all altered. In their place, I was transported to a world of nothingness, where all my truths were demolished, where I was forced to surrender or be destroyed.

By 'surrender', I mean letting go of everything that I knew to be true and falling into a chasm that was deep and foreign. This act of surrender changes you on the most profound level, disengaging you from the world as you know it and leading you to a place of no return. As the saying goes, 'In this world, but not of it.'

How you process all this defines the experience as a gift or a curse. Do you surrender to this experience and open yourself up to the unknown and all that may arise from it? Or do you seek escape through self-harm, drugs, alcohol or medication?

Without a doubt, for me, my love for my children kept me going—knowing that they needed me and I simply couldn't leave them. Alongside that there was faith. I was drawn to have faith in something that I couldn't see, feel, hear, smell or touch—something beyond anything that my five senses could comprehend. Faith in something that was so far outside my human experience that I had no words to describe it. It had no concept, no form, no substance. I was jumping out of a plane with no parachute.

This leap into the unknown can deliver you to a place of healthy nonattachment—as opposed to isolation—if you embrace it. I finally appreciated the Buddhists' use of 'non-attachment' as a definition of feeling whole and complete in oneself, allowing the ebb and flow of life without resistance or clinging. In love, it is respecting another's journey and embracing their energy in your life wholeheartedly, surrendering when necessary. This, in fact, allows us to love more fully, as it is not born from a need for anyone to complete us, but instead means sharing ourselves fully. No addiction, no drama, because we are complete and free from feeling the fear of losing love when we acquire it. The same applies to ego, identity, labels, titles, money—in fact, attachment of any kind.

It took me some time to understand this feeling and I initially experienced it as numbness and disconnection in some areas. My love of nature, animals, peace and quiet deepened. I continued to love and appreciate my work, caring for myself and my children. I never felt alone or lonely in these spaces, and they continued to hold meaning and purpose. Even when alone, I felt surrounded by energic forces that kept me company, feeling peaceful and divinely guided.

I did, however, feel shut down in other ways. For a period, joy, happiness, laughter, anticipation and excitement were distant emotions. I could recall them from the past, but could no longer feel them in the moment. I was driven by purpose, meaning and function. I still felt kindness and appreciation towards things, but also felt less connection.

Additionally, I often felt overwhelming loneliness and isolation around others at social events. Expressing joy or happiness felt like pressure, like a selfless act that I needed to perform so that others would feel comfortable. I went deeper inside myself while widening the smile on the outside.

As a result, social situations felt strained. Being social for its own sake felt as though it was taking me from something, as opposed to stepping out into something. Interactions felt a little predictable and the magic of meeting new people in a purely social way had vanished. I would often feel out of flow, out of alignment. Not in an introverted way; I had in fact never felt so confident and in-touch with who I was.

This was also not from a judgemental viewpoint; I appreciated every human being and I could see and appreciate their uniqueness. But I could no longer feel the meaning in a purely social interaction. I had no genuine response to it. Like I was observing human interaction without the experience of it, I could remember how these exchanges felt and mimicked them when necessary, but felt disengaged. My ability to connect on a personal level in these situations abandoned me.

I also felt so sensitive to energy. The energy could be greatly disturbing if it wasn't aligned with my own. I would watch people laughing and engaging freely with envy.

This state may have been an altered relationship with dopamine and cortisol after the intensity of what I had experienced. Perhaps I had flatlined after such extreme emotion and needed to heal, or maybe I was moving closer to non-attachment. Perhaps a combination of both.

The positive side of this was realising that I could feel people's emotions with increased clarity and intensity. I could read their state of health and was drawn to those facing challenges, wanting to help them work through it. I loved my work and would get lost in the complexity and uniqueness of each of my clients. It was an honour and a privilege to be allowed into their energetic space and contribute to their healing. It still is.

However, I started to feel a strange grief for the girl and woman I used to be. When I looked at old photos, I felt that I was looking at another lifetime lived by another person. This stirred a deep emptiness. At times I missed her terribly, like a lost friend.

Life can feel fragmented after unusual events, rather like a timeline split—the sort we feel after a pivotal event like an illness or accident, the death of a loved one, or even a wonderful change like a new baby. Life looks one way, then in an instant, looks and feels completely different.

Ascension can be similar. We may also end up with few people who carry the full story of our lives in their memory. In my case, new friends have appeared over the years, while most older ones have faded away. My work is wonderful, but my clients fully experience me in the now and know nothing of my former life. Parents age and have a fading memory of your past, and less ability to grasp the present. My children know me in my capacity as their mother, but have no real account of me as a girl, teenager or young woman before their birth.

We can feel somewhat defined by how we exist in the minds of others. The profound changes left me with no one in my life who shared my full journey from start to finish—from the 'before and after' of this experience.

I am still working through this grief, but it has given me enormous strength to stand alone, with some intangible energetic force by my side that knows me—that followed and coauthored my story and 'has my back'.

Whatever this indefinable presence is, it has taken hold in my life and leads me forward. No past, to define me. Just the now. It brought to light the importance of embracing inner strength and personal power while balancing it with humility.

One of the biggest battles for those experiencing ascension is traditional ideas of love, innocence, family and constancy sometimes being out of alignment with growth and evolution. I was personally left reflecting on the Buddhist saying that 'change is the only constant'—but this can leave you feeling like you're floating out at sea and in need of an anchor.

I came to the comforting thought that perhaps the constancy is in the *rhythm* of change. The rhythm of life in plants, animals and people, blooming for a cycle then passing and allowing for new life to continue the dance. The breathing in and breathing out of cycles in which we reflect, recalibrate, change, grow and look inward, then 'action' our changes in the world.

This is exciting—this is the lifeforce, but it can be in opposition to constancy. We may need our current relationships to alter or deepen to survive, or we may seek new relationships that resonate more deeply with our internal changes. We may require new professional pursuits. The law of rhythm and growth constantly guides us in every facet of our lives.

Perhaps therein lies the constant—in the pursuit, in the struggle and the journey. Striving to elevate, learn and create, to find god in whichever form it takes for that soul through these ever-changing cycles. This thought can stir compassion and deep honour for the human condition.

Harmony and peace sit not with 'nothing going wrong' but with having faith in oneself that we can tackle any issue, any challenge. That we are not alone in this universe but connected to divine guidance keeping us company along the way.

One of the markers of spiritual maturity may be the ability to sit with paradoxes, uncertainties and conflicts and still feel at ease because we know that nothing is certain. Everything is changing and in flux, we trust ourselves to work through it, and current stresses represent only a moment in time.

Ascension and you

What is ascension?

What is ascension exactly and why do we ascend at all? This is a complicated question and could be answered in myriad ways through the lenses of religious faiths, ancient beliefs, astrology, physics, quantum law, biology and spiritual perspectives.

What is certain is that living creatures are created to grow and evolve. Humans grow physically from baby to adult, grow in intellect through education and life experience, and evolve spiritually through living intuitively, through practices such as meditation and yoga, and by acquiring spiritual knowledge through study and prayer.

There is, however, an innate intelligence that has created us and every living organism in our multi-verse. We do not consciously make our heart beat or digest our food or instigate the autophagy of old cells to create new ones. We didn't design our neurology—our nervous, circulatory or respiratory system. Our bodies were designed for us. All of nature passes through seasonal cycles working synergistically with the greater ecosystem to continually renew and regenerate.

Spiritual and religious faiths are fundamentally built on the premise of a higher creative force. Yet we tend to exist on this planet feeling rather alone, isolated in our responsibility to play out the lives we have been given. Perhaps the ascension process being experienced by millions around the world attests to the fact that we are *not* alone.

We are in fact intrinsically linked to a creative force, regardless of the form this takes to the reader. Is it possible that it is time for this source energy to now work through us to evolve further into a new realm of being? Pushing life forward into the new age of enlightened, light-body souls who are not only living through their five senses, but harnessing their sixth sense in order to live a more spiritual existence?

As a global community, many are questioning the matrix of our reality, including our education system, control and manipulation of the media, and pharmaceutical medicine that is driven by profit, often undermining our innate ability to heal.

Add to this rampant consumerism, student loans, bank and tax debt that keep us bound and enslaved to the system. An allopathic healthcare system that rarely teaches practitioners and patients about food and a food industry that has no interest in health. Artificial colours, flavours, sweeteners, preservatives, rancid fats and sugar so often dominate the ingredients list of processed goods.

Religious teaching that is often grounded in fear, inequality, wrath and punishment, as opposed to true divinity and unconditional and eternal love.

What, then, is driving us to this heightened consciousness? This collective 'stepping back' to view the architecture of our human lives and question the architect behind it?

To reach this point is somewhat of an out-of-body experience in that we are looking for our truth—not conditioned indoctrinated truth, but our divine truth. A release from what is known, in order to explore the unknown. This introspection requires an elevation of the self beyond the five senses. A feeling that all is not well in the material world, that our liberation lies in the understanding of our spiritual entitlement. An entitlement for peace, health and freedom that exists beyond this earthly construct.

The road to these entitlements can be challenging. It requires a purging of old beliefs and internalised reactive responses from our mind, our cells, our very DNA. It requires of us the recognition that source energy works *through* us and not separate to us. That we must stand accountable and claim our right as divine creators, which honours the creative force that designed us for this purpose. Look at it, perhaps, like J.K. Rowling: we are running around like muggles, letting life happen to us instead of picking up our wands to manifest our reality with focus and intent.

It is interesting to note that this period of human ascension has been mentioned or alluded to in astrological, religious and esoteric texts.

Astrologically, it is widely agreed that we have entered the Age of Aquarius, which is said to be a time of deep reflection and transformation. Personal and collective identities are apt to shift and evolve during this time.

Not surprisingly, the Age of Aquarius holds a central theme of more open and diverse information and education. The internet has of course afforded us this medium, allowing a communal sharing of ideas, themes and concepts as opposed to the narrow views previously controlled and broadcast by mainstream media.

The ancient Mayan long-count calendar is estimated to have ended on 21 December 2012. Many in the western world interpreted this to mean world destruction. I remember on this day how news commentators, comedians, talk-show hosts and radio hosts joked about 'the end of the world'. One even conducted a comic countdown to a cataclysmic event that would end us all.

No such event occurred, of course. But perhaps this day marked a new cycle in the evolution of man.

According to some Christian scholars, many bible prophecies of the 'end times' are now unfolding, which will lead to the second coming of Christ. More spiritual, esoteric or gnostic beliefs reframe this as the resurrection of Christ consciousness within, which is consistent with awakening principles. A time to work in concert with powerful internal and external energies to purge the ego and resurrect the soul of infinite love and unity consciousness; a time to raise the vibration of ourselves and our planet.

Ascension is also attributed to the shifting from a three-dimensional realm to a five-dimensional realm, in which Earth is moving from a denser vibrational state to a higher vibrational state. This vibrational state represents higher consciousness, which recognises unity, unconditional love and creativity as opposed to ego, separation, competition and duality. Humans inhabiting the planet are required to hold this new frequency, to survive here and resonate with the new energy. The body is therefore required to cleanse and upgrade in preparation. Could this have been what the Mayans forecast by the ending of one calendar and the birthing of a new era?

Many have also developed an interest in quantum law and study the teachings of ancient mystics, or more recently works of Einstein, who stated that all is vibration, all is energy—consistent with the fifth dimensional paradigm. In this paradigm, creation shifts from the physical to the energetic, where thoughts, emotion and intentions align and project out to the quantum field where they vibrate as an energetic frequency.

This frequency has a magnetic quality that can then attract energy that is in alignment—be it people, experiences or opportunities. Therefore, in this realm, mastering the internal state is the key to manifesting desired outcomes.

It is crucial, however, to surrender the outcome of this manifestation to the universe, as we may not always have it delivered in a form that we anticipate. As the saying goes, 'I prayed to God for flowers, so he gave me rain.'

Solar flares are also cited by many in the spiritual community as a contributing factor for ascension. This is due to energetic changes they cause in the atmosphere and their impact on the human body.

A solar flare is a small explosion that releases energy, light and high-speed particles into space from the sun's surface. There are many texts and writings that allude to this powerful energy affecting our very DNA. Esoterically, all our DNA is recognised as holding our past memory from this or other lifetimes, in addition to our evolutionary potential.

Ascension symptoms

Ascension symptoms are many and varied. They can be experienced emotionally, psychologically and physically as every aspect of the human being is clearing, cleansing, purging, growing and expanding.

Ascension is uniquely experienced by each person. Understanding ascension and being open to the changes inherent in the process helps enormously. I was running blind, and no doubt went into shock in the early stages.

Knowledge truly is power. Understanding the inherent nature of ascension can provide stable ground and allow you to embrace the process, endure the difficulties and commit to the learning. It can even facilitate curiosity, surrender and courage.

Once again, please seek medical advice first to ensure that your symptoms are not due to any conditions that may require treatment.

Physical symptoms

Changing sleep patterns

You may have trouble falling or staying asleep, or wake throughout the night. You may still feel tired after waking up.

Brain activity

This may include headaches, severe head fog, pressure around the head and crown, or feeling like your brain is wired and can't shut down.

Changes in eating habits

You may lose or gain appetite or feel repulsed by foods you usually enjoy. You may experience cravings, sudden sensitivity or intolerances to certain foods, resulting in issues such as bloating or nausea.

Changes in weight or body composition

Your metabolism may increase or decrease, or you may see changes in bowel habits, amplified detoxification, sudden unexplained weight gain (particularly around the solar plexus area) or unexplained weight loss.

Changes in sight

This may include blurry vision, seeing shimmering or glittery particles, auras around people, plants or animals, or seeing things as transparent. When you close your eyes, you no longer see darkness, but colours or images and lights. You may see colours as particularly vivid or bright or have altered night vision.

Changes in hearing

You may have increased or decreased hearing, or hear sounds within the head such as alarms, beeping, static or music. Other sounds may include whistling, running water, bees buzzing, humming, wind blowing or ringing noises.

Enhanced sense of smell

This may make aromas more pleasurable or overwhelming, depending on the source.

Increased sensitivity to toxicity

This can include environmental toxins such as personal care items, household cleaners, petrol or perfumes. Or it can mean emotional toxicity such as aggression, violence, ego or manipulation.

Changes in the skin

You might have changes in skin texture, or experience rashes, acne, shingles or styes. The skin is a major detox pathway and will be helping to eliminate toxic build-up from the body.

Body changes and sensations

You may have extreme feelings of heat or cold. You may feel vibrational energy running through your body or electrical sensations. You may have changes in libido, strange sexual sensations, feelings of floating, out-of-body experiences or involuntary body movements. You may feel vibrations in your surroundings.

Changes in your energy levels

These can be quite extreme. You may feel like you could jump out of your skin and achieve limitless tasks one moment, then be enveloped with intense bodily fatigue the next.

Unexplained bruising and injury

This can vary in intensity, happen in different parts of the body and be one-off or recurring.

Flu-like symptoms

These can include headaches, diarrhea, constipation, nausea, vomiting, unexplained sweating, vertigo or dizziness, unexplained fevers or chills, chest pain, irregular heartbeat, body spasms and cramps, and general body aches.

Impact on electricity and machinery

People experiencing ascension may trigger electrical and mechanical malfunctions in their surrounds. The human body has an electromagnetic field known as the human bio-field. The frequency of this field is within the electromagnetic spectrum, but not visible to the human eye. The heightening electrical effect often experienced during the ascension process would explain its impact on surrounding electrical devices—not to mention other humans, who may feel 'electrified' and heightened (or drained) by that person's presence.

Cognitive changes

Cognitive changes can include challenges with memory or recalling language and words, and lack of concentration or patience with linear, dry communication such as spreadsheets, emails, documents or any complex information requiring analysis. You may have a general feeling of 'spaciness' and feel overwhelmed by tasks.

You may instead be drawn to the more creative mediums of expression. This could include photography, art, music, nature and animals, dance or movement, being creative with food, your garden, personal beauty or the beauty of your home. You may be looking to explore your sexuality or feel drawn to understand the human psyche more deeply through spiritual exploration—or even through books and movies depicting these themes. You are looking to awaken your senses, including your sixth sense of intuition. You are seeking inspiration.

The right hemisphere of the brain is responsible for psychic abilities, intuition, emotions, your ability to experience and appreciate your senses, and your creative vision. The left hemisphere is dedicated to more linear functions such as order, structure, sequencing, analysis, evaluation and problem-solving. As the ascension process requires you to release old information that dictated reactive thoughts, beliefs, ideas and general indoctrination in order to liberate you into your true essence, the left-brain function may take a back seat for a while.

The ultimate endeavour is that over time, your heart and your right brain take the lead, with the left brain free to support you with logic and discernment. Mastery of the two hemispheres supports optimal emotional and spiritual health.

Emotional symptoms

Extreme and varied waves of emotion

Your emotional range may be expanded, with intense, unpredictable feelings such as rage, frustration, fear, horror, love, compassion, grief, sadness, addiction and euphoria coming to the surface. These feelings can be ever-changing, and can be momentary or longer term. They can relate to expansion of the heart chakra, letting go of repressed feelings, or trauma from this lifetime or past lifetimes.

Changes in personal truth

As a result of these repressed feelings and emotions emerging and releasing, you may search for a new homeostasis within, question old patterns of belief and fixed ideas about what defines you and the life you wish to live. In its place you may develop a renewed sense of self-esteem and self-worth.

This can sometimes be accompanied by an unsettling sense that your life feels forever altered—that you have left your old self behind. The future feels impossible to imagine as it exists in a realm which cannot be defined by anything from the past. Your creative and personal powers feel ignited and embraced, but sometimes with nowhere to put them in the present moment.

You may also begin to question others in your immediate world and in the wider matrix to which you have attached yourself. It is crucial during this time to seek support and guidance to ensure that you fully explore the deeper meaning of these changes before making life-altering decisions.

Overwhelming drive for change

Relationships, your work or profession, the home you live in, or the state or country you inhabit may no longer serve you. The changes derived from this growth are explosive and can affect all aspects of your life.

You may feel an overwhelming urge to purge restrictive habits and routines and find your life purpose. This can lead to impulsive decisions if not managed. Be patient, and gain knowledge and perspective, so that changes you embrace align you with your ultimate path.

Social change

A change in your vibrational frequency may put you out of balance with current relationships. In addition, your role within those relationships simply may not resonate any longer. You may wish to cut ties with certain people and avoid certain social interactions, or you may find you need to assert yourself and express your truth to others.

By being more authentic, some relationships will naturally come to an end, while others will gravitate towards you. You may also feel the need to spend more time in solitude to self-reflect.

Feeling close to nature

Many people experiencing ascension express a deepened understanding and connection with nature and their place in the natural world. They feel more in-tune with seasonal cycles and circadian rhythms. They may feel closer to animals and able to communicate with them. Colours may look brighter and the miracle and beauty of all life forms can be deeply appreciated. Many people feel sensitivity to weather changes.

Changing internal pace

Time may feel like it is speeding up and you are moving through personal issues rapidly. As you are tuning in with what resonates with you, you may develop greater clarity in your vision for the future.

You may find a sudden passion or spiritual pursuit and be suddenly hungry for knowledge and growth on this subject. Books, movies or people may suddenly appear at your doorstep as life teachers. They may be there to enlighten or to assist in bringing the negative to the surface, for you to recognise what needs to be purged and cleared from your system. You may become extremely aware of coincidences and synchronistic events that are leading you on your journey. You may feel divinely guided and watched over.

Be mindful through this period to ensure that any change of internal pace does not create impatience or disillusionment with the outside world. This is a wonderful time of accelerated learning, but it is imperative to ground yourself in the beauty of the day-to-day. That is, the small interactions with loved ones, being around nature, gratitude for food and comfort, and feeling blessed for this inner growth.

Tuning in with psychic abilities

This can include receiving information energetically, feeling, seeing or hearing things not necessarily available in the immediate environment, heightened perception, receiving 'downloads' of information, feeling that time is speeding up or slowing down, or sensing or seeing other energetic beings around you, particularly at night, or have the sensation of being touched or spoken to. Hold the knowledge that light is infinitely more powerful than dark, and your absence of fear will block negative energies. Invite the light in to guide you.

Symbols

Symbols, divine geometry and patterns or numeral sequences may suddenly catch your attention. You may see a depth and meaning in them for the first time and feel the messages or inspiration that they may be sending you. Honour these clues and allow them to lead you on your path. Feel inspired and know that all thoughts are prayer.

Self-care

Self-care through ascension is critical. You may be challenged and psychologically disoriented in ways you are not prepared for. This section of the book describes some helpful coping mechanisms.

Being comfortable with feeling uncomfortable

Human beings are designed to seek pleasure. At its most primal, this keeps us alive by telling the brain that we are relaxed, abundant and safe. As cave-people we sought food, shelter, safety and companionship to release oxytocin, dopamine, serotonin and other feel-good hormones that signal all is well with the world.

However, in a more complex situation such as ascension, we need to recognise that what may traditionally be seen as negative emotions are in fact serving us as a possible means to an end. The end being growth, resilience, gratitude, increased empathy and compassion, which can only be gained through some suffering and hardship.

We should embrace and welcome all difficulties as challenges and opportunities for such growth. We simply 'don't know what we don't know' and life can throw situations in our path to test and empower us in a way that our past experience provides no reference for.

Ascension can provide an extreme example of this. All the physical pain and psychological agony, the fear of the unknown energies that spring forth from our very selves, have no point of reference. It is the complete unknown, plunging us into an abyss of uncertainty, no relationship left untouched—including our relationship with ourselves. Trust and surrender are our only course.

Honouring this process—balancing feeling with logic, human with divine—is crucial. Detach from what you 'know' and allow the unknown to enter your world while grounding into your human responsibilities and relationships with love and gratitude. Find a counsellor or mentor to help you navigate the process. Seek ways to feel comfortable with being uncomfortable.

Intelligence is not measured solely by the accrual of information. The ability to concentrate, retain and apply information is important and displays sound cognitive function. However, intelligence is a fluid process; it is dynamic and engaging, and I believe that cognitive flexibility works hand in hand with cognitive capacity.

The ability to open our minds to new concepts, feelings and experiences is essential to continually broaden our neural networks and allow growth. Awakening demands this of us: to survive ascension, an ability to allow space in our brain and in our being for the unknown is critical. Otherwise, the result can be cognitive dissonance, heightened anxiety—even hysteria. So be open to what you don't know and allow the empty space to enter you and to expand you in ways you never thought possible.

Some helpful practices may include:

- journalling thoughts, feelings, dreams and experiences
- deepening your understanding of the ascension process through study and research
- reaching out for a personal mentor or a community who understands the process
- practising non-resistance.

Build an awareness of your habits, thoughts, beliefs and internal dialogue (inner voice). Witness them and challenge them where necessary. Open your mind and heart to freedom and change and release yourself from old, indoctrinated, learned, rote behaviour.

Meditation

Meditation can assist by quieting the mind. While we are 'thinking' we are primarily in the left hemisphere and replaying old, learned behaviour. The aim of meditation is to clear the mind, allowing new sensations and revelations to enter our being.

On a physical level, meditation helps move the body away from the sympathetic nervous system (fight-or-flight) back to the parasympathetic (rest-and-digest) mode, which regulates and calm the emotions.

Meditation is also the practice of simply being present. Before my ascension journey began, I would often go for my daily walk, then return home or to my car and recall nothing at all from the walk. I was so lost in my thoughts that the beauty of the beach or park was lost to me.

I believe that being present is a component of being grateful. When we are present for a friend or loved one, we are showing gratitude for their presence. Watering plants while admiring their beauty or feeding and cuddling our pets with mindful gratitude of their love and devotion is gratitude. However, so often we carry these things out while distracted or annoyed by the chore.

Cooking beautiful food with gratitude is meditation. Eating mindfully and enjoying all the tastes and textures fully is meditation. That warm luxurious shower in the morning can be meditation.

It truly can be applied to all areas of our lives. We never really know that we're in the 'good old days' until they pass. We are in them right now. So the *first* meditation is living with mindful gratitude and being present for all that life has to offer.

We also have more structured meditations available to us. They can be simple, but can create powerful shifts over time. The three outlined below are my favourite practices, but there are an almost infinite supply to discover in books or online.

You may prefer to source a guided meditation or complement one of the below with background sound such as Tibetan bowls, chanting, birds, rain, running water or soft meditation music.

My three favourite meditations

The first two meditations here relate to the chakras. Chakra means 'wheel' and refers to spinning energy points in your body. Chakras correspond to bundles of nerves, organs and areas of our energetic body that affect emotional and physical wellbeing. They are junction points between our physiology and consciousness.

There are seven primary chakras that run along your spine. Each of these main chakras has a corresponding name, colour and area of the spine, from the sacrum to the crown of the head. For optimal physical and emotional health, these chakras should be open, aligned and balanced.

The seven chakras

Root chakra
Location: Base of spine
Colour: Red
Represents: Core survival needs, grounding, security, stability, trust in receiving abundance
Associated with: Adrenal glands, kidneys, lower spine and sense of smell

Sacral chakra
Location: Below the navel
Colour: Orange
Represents: Sexuality, reproduction, relationship to the masculine/feminine and creative expression
Associated with: Reproductive organs and sense of taste

Solar plexus
Location: Stomach

Colour: Yellow
Represents: Self-identity, personal power and esteem, inner compass, will, the ability to 'digest' life
Associated with: Stomach and intestines, liver, gallbladder, spleen and sense of sight

Heart chakra

Location: Chest area
Colour: Green
Represents: Love, including self-love, compassion, connection, wisdom, faith, devotion, intuition
Associated with: Respiratory and immune system and the sense of touch

Throat chakra

Location: Throat
Colour: Blue
Represents: Communication and truthful self-expression, clarity, will, authenticity, knowledge, sharing and connection with others
Associated with: Thyroid, lungs, respiratory system and sense of sound

Third-eye chakra

Location: On the forehead between the eyes
Colour: Indigo
Represents: Intuition, insight, realisation, sensing beyond the five senses, spiritual awareness and enlightenment
Associated with: Pineal and pituitary gland and endocrine system

Crown chakra

Location: Centre top of the skull
Colour: Gold or white
Represents: Connection to the divine, source energy, union, unbounded awareness, enlightenment

Associated with: The nervous system

Meditation 1

Find a comfortable position—in bed, in a garden or park, on the beach or simply on the floor—and close your eyes. Breathe slowly and deeply through your nose and out of your mouth through the entire meditation.

See an endless golden cord emanating from the top of your head (crown chakra) and connecting with the divine, your future evolution, the unknown. Think of this as universal source energy guiding you daily, working through you and for you. Feel a connection to the sun, moon, stars and limitless space.

Next, see a red cord emanating from your root chakra (lower back), grounding roots deep into the earth, which nourishes you in your human form and expression, establishing a deep rich connection with Mother Earth. Feel a connection to the ocean, the land and all living creatures.

Feel love and gratitude for the guidance from above and the opportunity to experience life in your human body on Earth.

Meditation 2

Find a comfortable position—in bed, in a garden or park, on the beach or simply on the floor—and close your eyes. Breathe slowly and deeply through your nose and out of your mouth through the entire meditation.

Allow your attention to gently settle on your root chakra. See the colour red and say the words:

I am one with Gaia. My spirit is connected through my body to nature. I trust the process of life and allow it to unfold, feeling safe, secure and protected in my human body by Mother Earth.

Feel these words deeply and repeat five to ten times.

Allow your attention to gently settle on your sacral chakra, see the colour orange and say the words:

I have the god/goddess energy running through me. I am radiant, vital, beautiful and sensual. I create freely and live my life with passion.

Feel these words deeply and repeat five to ten times.

Allow your attention to gently settle on your solar plexus. See the colour yellow and say the words:

I accept life as it is, knowing that the power sits in my response. I am the creator of my life and embrace all experiences as gained knowledge. I live my life with passion and purpose and feel empowered and confident to act in alignment with my truth and manifest my desires.

Feel these words deeply and repeat five to ten times.

Allow your attention to gently settle on your heart chakra. See the colour green and say the words:

I love and honour myself deeply. I choose to give and receive love as an expression of my inner truth. I have faith, inner harmony and devotion to the power of unconditional love. I feel joy, bliss and peace because my love is unconditional and balanced with discernment. I am loved by a higher power.

Feel these words deeply and repeat five to ten times.

Allow your attention to gently settle on your throat chakra. See the colour blue and say the words:

My voice is truthful and strong. I speak with ease and clarity. I communicate from my highest self with love and confidence. My voice carries my love, intention, will and wisdom into the world and is an instrument of manifestation.

Feel these words deeply and repeat five to ten times.

Allow your attention to gently settle on your third-eye chakra. See the colour indigo and say the words:

I connect with the world beyond my five senses. My intuition and feelings tune me into universal truth and wisdom. My visions are clear and my imagination radiant with possibility. I am fully present and aware in each moment. I trust my instincts and listen to the quiet voice of my soul.

Feel these words deeply and repeat five to ten times.

Finally, allow your attention to gently settle on your crown chakra. See gold and white light and say the words:

I am a soul having a human experience. I am endless and eternal, pure love and light, a direct extension of divine source energy. Everything I need is within me and guided by source for my evolution and highest purpose. My intention and desires align with cosmic will.

Feel these words deeply and repeat five to ten times.

Gently bring your awareness back to your surroundings.

Balancing your chakra energy is a simple way to bring awareness, honour and healing to the various aspects of your human and spiritual self.

Meditation 3

The most critical requirement for human life is oxygen. Oxygen is primarily taken in through the breath, so as you work through this meditation, pay particular attention to the slow and steady rhythm of your breath.

Find a comfortable position—in bed, in a garden or park, on the beach or simply on the floor—and close your eyes. Breathe slowly and deeply through your nose and out of your mouth through the entire meditation.

Feel yourself as pure light moving through a dense forest, breathing life-giving oxygen into your energy. Breathe in the greenery and the smell of rain-covered plants and established trees. Feel their wisdom and cherish the animals that live here. See this oxygen emanating from the forest clear away all old cellular material and birth light, healthy, clear cells within you that nourish and support your system.

Next, feel yourself as pure light moving beside the ocean, breathing life-giving oxygen into your energy. Breathe in the salt and sea air and marvel at its power and beauty. Cherish the sea life that lives here. See the oxygen emanating from the ocean clear away all old cellular material and re-birth light, healthy, clear cells that nourish and support your system.

Feel yourself as pure floating light, free from the need for anything that does not serve you. You are created to be your highest self and you invite in only that which nourishes and supports this journey. Feel the power in this decision.

Physical health

We were designed to live primarily outdoors, on bare feet, eating from nature's harvest. Yet we now spend most of our time indoors. Over the past three decades we have been increasingly sitting or lying while working on computers or scrolling on phones.

Meanwhile, many of us are addicted to the chemicals in processed food, or to alcohol or recreational or pharmaceutical drugs. Over the past three decades working in wellness, I have witnessed technology joining that list of addictions, with phones, tablets and computers becoming our core focus. We now live looking inwards (fed a warped, algorithmic version of our tastes and interests) instead of outwards.

Additionally, the stress hormone cortisol has become an addiction for many. This is, after all, a steroid hormone, releasing adrenaline into the system. This can lead us to create dramas in our lives to get the 'buzz' from that shot of cortisol. In the current world, a calm orderly life can be viewed as dull and somehow lacking.

These addictions are so often tools of avoidance, distracting us from our deeper selves. Freeing our body and mind of these substances and activities forces us to face our psychological and physical wellbeing and work through what is challenging and in need of our attention and repair. It awakens us from a sleep and is an essential part of the ascension process.

Overall physical health needs to be optimised to facilitate the ascension process. There is no doubt that I felt more comfortable having undergone testing for all the possible physical causes of my suffering. This is imperative before focusing on ascension as the cause of physical or emotional change.

Speak to a qualified physician about your symptoms. They can suggest specific testing, such as blood, urine, saliva, breath or faecal testing to discount certain conditions. They can also order allergy tests if needed. Once your baseline physiology is understood, a personal protocol can be put into place to ensure optimal health based on your specific needs.

There are, however, four vital basic elements for health which will not only support you through your ascension process but also facilitate improved all-round health for you and your family.

These four (described in more detail below) are:

- oxygen
- water
- food—nourishment
- movement.

Through the ascension process, when the body is doing profound purging, healing and transitioning, the quality of these elements is crucial.

Oxygen

Oxygen is the primary element required for human life, followed closely by water. Oxygen is primarily obtained through the breath. Conscious deep breathing is the best practice you can embrace to maximise your intake. Breathing in through the nose deeply into the diaphragm is the most efficient way to breathe as it draws down on the lungs, creating negative pressure in the chest, resulting in improved air flow. Most people shallow-breathe into the chest, which is less effective. (It is interesting to watch babies and children as they instinctively breathe correctly.)

Breathing out to release carbon dioxide is as important as the in-breath. I practise and teach the five-five-five method: breathing in for five slow beats, holding for five then releasing for five, until the lungs feel completely empty.

Unfortunately, indoor and outdoor air quality has been compromised, so it is important to spend time in areas that are oxygen-rich, such as parks, forests and the ocean if possible. Ensure that your home is well ventilated and consider running an air purifier overnight where you sleep.

Certain food can also help oxygenate the body. Dairy products, meat and eggs provide oxygen-boosting components, as do green and cruciferous vegetables, nuts, seeds, beetroot and legumes. Some excellent fruits include citrus, avocados, pomegranates, kiwi and berries. All foods that are rich in iron and nitrates are particularly effective at transporting oxygen throughout the body. Choose organic and sun-ripened produce whenever possible.

Water

Water is the second most essential element to human life. It makes up approximately 60% of total body weight and supports virtually every system in the body. Water acts as a transport system delivering oxygen and nutrients to cells, lubricates and protects organs, provides moisture for the eyes, nose, mouth and digestive tract. Water aids in metabolism, stamina, cognitive function, waste removal and temperature regulation. It also balances electrolytes and helps maintain healthy blood levels.

Municipal water supplies carry a heavy toxic load including chemicals, pesticides, heavy metals, chlorine and fluoride so tap water should be avoided. There are excellent filters available, however most recommended is a reverse osmosis system which ensures that fluoride is removed also.

Store water in glass containers as opposed to plastic whenever possible.

Aim to drink 1.5 to 2 litres daily, preferably between meals, adding some lemon or lime if desired, for taste and vitamin C. Adding a tiny pinch of Himalayan rock or Celtic Sea salt also assists in delivering hydration to the cells and mineralises the body.

You can also boost hydration through food high in water, including raw fruits and vegetables, quality bone broth, smoothies and drinks such as herbal tea.

Food

Our food supply has become remarkably complicated. We are dealing with genetically modified crops, trans fats, seed oils, and artificial colours, preservatives and flavours. Foods that are so processed our bodies don't even have enzymes to break them down. Sugar, table salt, thickeners, flavour enhancers, artificial sweeteners, MSG. The list goes on and on.

Our bodies are designed for food provided by nature, so a primal diet is ideal. Additionally, we need to consider the source of that food. Am I eating a chicken that has been raised in a pasture, fed a natural diet and allowed to roam free—or one raised in a cage inside a factory, pumped full of steroids and antibiotics? Is my fish farmed or ocean caught? Have my fruit and vegetables ripened in the sun, or under warehouse lights? Is my produce organic, or has it been soaked in glyphosate and other pesticides?

The solution is to aim to eat whole food from nature: fruits, vegetables, nuts, seeds and legumes, organic wherever possible. Also focus on pasture-raised, grass-fed and finished meats and dairy, quality oils and fats such as nuts, fresh avocado, grass-fed ghee and butter, and organic olive and coconut oil.

Movement

Our bodies are designed to move daily. A combination of cardio, weight resistance and stretching are ideal. This may mean a run, walk or bike ride followed by some weightlifting for resistance then stretching to follow. Listen to your body's needs as you go through ascension and try to pick movement that feels good to you and provides some joy and release.

Movement is imperative for the circulation of blood. Adequate blood flow ensures oxygen delivery and transportation of nutrients throughout the body. It assists with hormone distribution, temperature regulation, immune system function, healing and removal of waste products from the system.

Movement builds muscle, protects bone density, keeps fascia supple and keeps the lymphatic system fluid.

Try to incorporate the outdoors into your routine to ensure some sensible sun exposure and grounding to maximise the benefits. Grounding connects us to the Earth's energy and is a vital factor in robust health and healing. It can reduce pain and inflammation, help to regulate our stress response, modulate mood, and improve sleep quality and overall vitality.

Grounding on earth and sand is ideal.

Incorporating some of these simple practices into your day will help keep your body functioning well. A healthier body will be more resilient to some of the stresses that can be brought on by the ascension process, such as increased autophagy of cells, dealing with sudden change, ascension flu-like symptoms and sleep deprivation.

Your journey

The miracle of evolution seemingly lies in surrendering one's self while also taking full ownership.

It is the interplay between the soul's infinite journey and our present-time human experience. That is, to be in-touch with our highest self—spirit self—yet ground this through our 'human suit', our earthly flesh-and-blood self.

This seems to be part of the art of living and one of our highest callings—the ability of surrender to the moment, fully present while also letting go, with no attachment to past labels, beliefs or old internal narratives.

In its ultimate form, ascension takes us to a place of unity consciousness. We recognise our need to use the ego (separate self) as a driving force to experience and create on this planet while understanding its place in the collective. And we express ourselves fully while showing compassion, love, regard and honour for all life around us, knowing that to injure other people, animals or our planet is to injure ourselves.

As we are both physical and vibrational beings, this begins with our ability to balance our physical with our vibrational frequency. To wear our human suit while aligning with our higher spiritual, ethereal selves. Heart with mind, soul with body.

In this state, we live and create with compassion and love. We practise nonattachment, ensuring that we draw things into our lives with the intention to show love and to leave it in an elevated state—not to use it to fill a void in ourselves or control it to feed the ego.

We graduate to feelings of joy and love, surrendering when necessary, always mindful of what is best for the collective moving forward.

We feel a sense of peace knowing that we are never alone. We become stronger and clearer in body, mind and soul, in alignment with our higher selves and highest intentions and purpose. We forgive ourselves and others along the way for error, for we recognise that we are here not to be perfect but to seek perfection, and it is through the seeking that we evolve and ascend.

Be brave through this process. Seek meaning in its profound teaching. I wish you joy and a life built from love.

Sharon Rush

www.ascensionwellness.com.au

9 781764 555609